MW00897376

This Book Belongs To:

_____

MOMENTS WITH
JESUS
ENCOUNTER BIBLE

© Copyright 2021—Bill Johnson and Eugene Luning

All rights reserved. This book is protected by the copyright laws of the United States of America. This book may not be copied or reprinted for commercial gain or profit. The use of short quotations or occasional page copying for personal or group study is permitted and encouraged. Permission will be granted upon request. Unless otherwise identified, Scripture quotations are taken from the HOLY BIBLE, NEW INTERNATIONAL VERSION®, Copyright © 1973, 1978, 1984, 2011 International Bible Society. Used by permission of Zondervan. All rights reserved. Scripture quotations marked NLT are taken from the Holy Bible, New Living Translation, copyright 1996, 2004, 2015. Used by permission of Tyndale House Publishers Inc., Wheaton, Illinois 60189. All rights reserved. All emphasis within Scripture quotations is the author's own. Please note that Destiny Image's publishing style capitalizes certain pronouns in Scripture that refer to the Father, Son, and Holy Spirit, and may differ from some publishers' styles.

DESTINY IMAGE® PUBLISHERS, INC.
P.O. Box 310, Shippensburg, PA 17257-0310

"Promoting Inspired Lives."

This book and all other Destiny Image and Destiny Image Fiction books are available at Christian bookstores and distributors worldwide.

Illustrations by Kevin and Kristen Howdeshell

For more information on foreign distributors, call 717 532-3040.

Reach us on the Internet: www.destinyimage.com.

ISBN 13: 978-0-7684-5610-3

ISBN 13 eBook: 978-0-7684-5611-0

ISBN TP Int'l: 978-0-7684-6013-1

For Worldwide Distribution, Printed in the U.S.A.

2 3 4 5 6 7 8 / 25 24 23 22 21

MOMENTS WITH
JESUS
ENCOUNTER BIBLE

20 *Immersive Stories from the Four Gospels*

Bill Johnson

Eugene Luning

Illustrated by Kristen & Kevin Howdeshell

Acknowledgements

Eugene Luning

My heart is full of gratitude to so many. To Bill—for his wonderful words and work on this project. To Kevin and Kristen—for "seeing" Jesus with such selfsame eyes. To the whole team at Destiny Image—for believing that we could bring Him to life in fresh new ways. To Christian—for being the greatest encourager I have ever known.

And thank you to the Anchor fellowship, here in Colorado, for letting me experiment for so many years with this particular style and voice. Thank you to Adam, Mike and Marvin for being visionaries and "arsonists" on behalf of the Other Country. Thank you to Young Life for being the first ministry who trusted me to speak of Jesus.

And thank you to Hadley, Tripp and Hoyt—you are the finest young followers of Jesus I know.

And thank you to my Jenny—for traveling all this way on the Way with me—you are the finest person that I know. I love you and I love you.

Kevin & Kristen Howdeshell

Thank you to Christian and Eugene for trusting us with the illustrations and for giving us much creative freedom.

Contents

A Word to Parents

From Bill Johnson

Jesus often gave natural lessons that had spiritual implications. For example, when He spoke in parables about the harvest, He was using a natural reality that His listeners would have been familiar with in order to teach them about a superior one in the spiritual world (see Matt. 13). Likewise, husbands and wives are to love one another (see Eph. 5). That is absolutely true in the natural. But the united family is also prophetic imagery for Jesus' love for His Bride, the Church. The structure and commitment of the earthly family speaks prophetically of what it means to be a part of the family of God.

The prayer that Jesus taught to His disciples began with the words, "Our Father." We are united under the family of God—brothers and sisters in Christ, who raise up sons and daughters. Every expression of His kingdom, every manifestation of His will on the earth, reveals itself within the context of family. Once you leave the concept of family life—the relational aspect of God's nature—you have left the subject of the kingdom.

When I was a young father, I spent the majority of my prayer and Bible-study time devoted to discovering what the Scriptures had to say about being a good husband and father. As a priority for a pastor, that might sound strange to some, but those were the topics that consumed my time and focus with the Lord. I knew that my family was the first and most important church I would ever pastor. So, I wanted to know what the Lord had to say about family. I didn't want to succeed in ministry but fail at home. I didn't want to impact crowds without impacting my own children.

We began to develop this culture within our home by nurturing each one of our children's personal relationship with God. Each child is unique. What worked for my boys didn't work for my daughter. Remember, the Bible says that we are to raise up each child "in the way that he should go" (Prov. 22:6). It doesn't say that we are to raise up our children in the ways *we think* they should go. We have the honor of stewarding the destinies and futures of individuals who have been uniquely designed by the Creator of the universe to impact the world for His glory. There's no better setting than the home to teach children about God's heart for them.

Cultivating your child's intimacy with God, however, will not happen by accident. The busyness of life tends to invade all of our good intentions. The most important things have to be intentionally scheduled; otherwise, as various things begin to pull on us, we will lose sight of the important role we play in our children's lives. Tools such as this Encounter Bible allow parents and grandparents to engage with children in a purposeful way. We will never regret sowing time into facilitating our children's relationship with God.

Beni and I tried to cultivate our kids' connection to God in a variety of ways. We expected our children to hear God's voice, so they learned to expect it as well. We tried not to make it a spooky, intense ordeal for them but rather simply invited them to listen to God's voice frequently, but without pressure. We would be in a small group with both children and adults, and I would say, "Tell me what you think God's doing in their life" pointing to someone in the room. Children would often speak with clarity and insight, bringing great encouragement to that individual. We were training them to hear God and speak from their conviction. Eventually, it became very natural for them.

We also invited them into our own relational journey with the Lord. I remember several times through their growing-up years when I became upset at something or was disrespectful to someone—maybe one of the kids or the guy driving the car that had just cut me off. I would confess to the whole family and have my kids lay hands on me and pray for me. We invited them to experience our conviction, but also participate in our repentance and forgiveness as we pursued the Holy Spirit in our daily lives.

They began to understand that everything in our lives rotated around our value for the presence of God. They witnessed our prayer and Bible-reading times, our worship, our mistakes, and our victories as we matured in Christ. And we made a point of bringing awareness to their growth as well. When one of them would honor or serve the other, I would stop them, saying, "Do you know what that was?" They would look up at me as though they were in trouble. But I would say, "That was a fruit of the Spirit. That was kindness. It is an evidence of the Holy Spirit working in your life. I'm so proud of you. Good job."

We have the incredible responsibility of demonstrating what God and His world are like when we raise our children and grandchildren. As parents, we rule our homes for the purpose of protection, but we also serve with the purpose of empowering our children. We want to release young people into their destiny. That is the privilege of parenting.

Our book, *Moments with Jesus,* invites your children or grandchildren to powerfully encounter the Jesus who worked miracles, spread hope, and joyfully blessed children, knowing each of them by name. In these pages, they will get to imagine what it would have felt like to be standing next to the Son of God, the Son of Man. Through engaging storytelling, the children in your life will be able to feel for themselves the incredible truths of the gospel: God sees and knows them, Jesus chose them and sacrificed everything for them to be with Him for eternity. The kind of atmosphere created by these insights inspire children to dream the dreams that bring glory to God. With that as their foundation, our children will be ready to take on any giant that comes their way.

Bill Johnson,
Bethel Church, Redding, CA

Chapter 1

The Beginning

Luke 2:8-20

Imagine lying on your back in the freshest, greenest grass. Overhead, the night sky spreads from edge to edge of your view: millions of twinkling, sparkling stars dot the darkness of a moonless night. You take a deep breath in, smelling all the smells of the grass and the wildflowers and the earth and the herd of sheep asleep nearby. You are very nearly asleep now yourself, hearing only the conversation of your friends, the fire crackling, the gust of a breeze blowing by...

That's when your view is suddenly lit up by a man! But, *Is he a man?* you wonder to yourself.

He stands just beyond the campfire and now he's blinding your eyes with light; he is looking right in your direction—at you and your friends.

"Do not be afraid!" he says, in a booming, almost overwhelming voice. "Listen, I bring you glorious news of great joy which is for all the people. This very day, in David's town, a Savior has been born for you. He is Christ, the Lord. Let this prove it to you: you will find a baby, wrapped up and lying in a manger."

Your heart is racing in your chest now. Your eyes are wide: you have never heard or seen anything quite like this...

Suddenly, overhead the sky—just a moment ago dark and dotted with a million stars—is now *invaded by the Army of Heaven!* Shoulder to shoulder, it's like they're marching from the throne room of Heaven—glowing with the fire of a thousand suns—and you press into the earth, trying to avoid their advance.

But with joy they begin to trumpet and shout for all to hear—for you to hear: "Glory to God in the highest Heaven! Peace on earth among men of good hearts!"

And then—just like that—with the thundering sound of their worship still ringing in your ears,

with the grass still bending under the blowing of their trumpets...

17

They're gone.

You look around. Your friends are all pressed down into the earth, frightened and amazed like you, but everything else is darkness again. The millions of twinkling, sparkling stars are back to dotting the darkness of the moonless night; the only sound is the fire's popping and crackling.

You stand up. Your heart continues to race. You say to your friends, "Let's get going to Bethlehem and see this thing that the Lord has made known to us!"

And so away you go...

journeying off over the darkened hills,

crossing streams and meadows, and walking beneath the spreading trees...

Until, stooping your head to get in through the opening of a hillside into the stable it holds, you lock eyes with a young mother and father inside. Your eyes take a moment to adjust to the dim lamplight within...

And there He is. The most powerful person in all human history—the mighty General of that Angel Army—who is laying, swaddled, on a bed of hay.

A baby. In a manger.

He slightly turns His head and your eyes meet for a moment. You fall to your knees and you worship this Christ, your Lord.

The invasion has begun. Glory to God in the highest Heaven!

Let's Talk About It

How do you think you would have felt if you had been one of the shepherds?

What do you think baby Jesus would have looked like?

Have you ever seen an angel? What do you think an army of Heaven would look like?

Chapter 2

An Evening at the River

Matthew 3:1-17, Mark 1:1-11, Luke 3:1-22

Imagine standing in the waters of a gently flowing river, up to your knees, feeling the coolness of the current passing you by. On both sides of the river, golden-brown hills rise and then fall; the edge of the riverbank is shaded by branches and leaves swirling in the wind. It is very nearly sunset time now. You have been standing at the edge of the waters almost all day long; finally, just a moment ago, you kicked off your sandals and waded into the river. The red and orange colors of dusk are beginning to rise; the waters look almost green now; you close your eyes and enjoy the peaceful sound of their flowing...

You are waiting to be baptized by the Baptist. The man named John. The son of Zechariah, the old Levite. Looking around, you watch the faces of all the other people in the crowds; they are looking happy and hopeful, joyful, and, also, a little serious. They are serious because John the Baptist, the man standing before you in the river, the one in ragged camel's skin, is calling you all into a new life. He is saying that the old things have gone away forever now; the new thing is coming—and coming *very soon*, he says.

In some ways, John the Baptist scares you. He scares you because his hair is standing on end—he eats wild locusts, you've heard—and, mostly, he scares you because of the look in his eyes.

The eyes of John the Baptist are wild. They speak of wilderness places, living in caves, great dangerous distances; and yet they also speak with the power and goodness of Heaven itself. The reason you have come to the river to hear from John, to be baptized by John, is because you want to know what Heaven is like...

Suddenly, John stops talking.

He stands up straight.

Everyone grows quiet as they watch his face change. He is looking over your shoulder, just behind you, and you turn to look. You see the Man John the Baptist is looking at.

This Man is dressed like any other man: cloak, tunic, belt and a worn-out pair of sandals on His dusty feet. He walks through the crowd just like any other man would walk through a crowd: there is nothing special in the way He's coming forward.

Oh, but His face, His look, *His eyes!* They are serious but laughing, kind but powerful, intense but as gentle as a happy lamb's would look.

You watch Him as He passes past the last of the crowd on the bank, kicking away His sandals, and entering the water in your direction. And here He comes... He brushes right against you and you catch His smell: the smell of the workshop, of carpentry. Then He's past you in the direction of John.

John is bowing his head as the Man approaches. The whole crowd is quiet—watching, waiting. John the Baptist and the Man whisper a few words to each other and then—just like everyone else—the Man is baptized by him. He rests Himself against the arms of John and then John lowers Him into the water and then—*SPLASH!*—He rises again...

Except...

suddenly, something is happening.

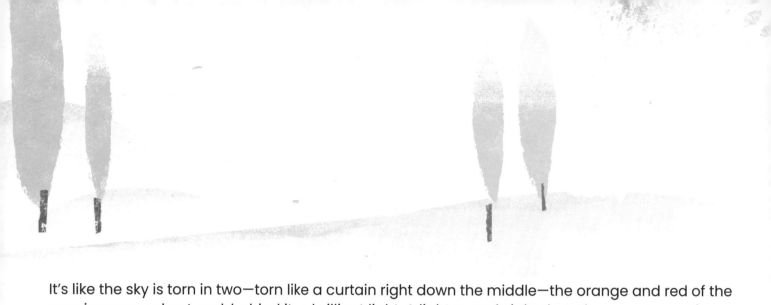

It's like the sky is torn in two—torn like a curtain right down the middle—the orange and red of the evening opened out and, behind it, a brilliant light. A light more bright than the sun at noontime on an August day.

You can't believe what you are seeing!

And out of that brilliant light, a bird—a dove—comes flying down over the hills, over the trees, over the river, and lands on the Man. It rests upon His shoulder and then it... disappears.

And suddenly the ground around you starts to shake and quake at the sound of a voice from out of Heaven:

"This is my dearly loved Son,
in whom my heart is pleased."

You would be terribly frightened by all of this—that torn sky, the heavenly dove, that booming voice—if you weren't so caught up in the Man. For He is looking in your direction now. And you can't stop looking at those wonderful eyes of His.

Let's Talk About It

Have you been baptized? Was it in a river, like the story, or was it someplace else? What do you think happened when you were baptized?

Draw a picture or describe what you think Jesus looked like.

What do you think God is saying about you right now? What kinds of things does He love about you? What do you think pleases Him about who you are?

Chapter 3

The Night of the Wedding

John 2:1-11

Imagine being a guest at a beautiful wedding party. You spent the whole afternoon buying a present, getting ready, and getting dressed. You are looking your absolute best as you watch the ceremony. The bride and groom are people you know and love very much; they are as happy as any two people could ever be. Your whole town is here to celebrate with them. And now that beautiful bride and handsome groom kiss—*they are married now!*—everyone is ready to head to the party and let loose...

And what a party it is, by the way! As you're walking into the courtyard of the house of the bride's family, you are looking around in amazement at all the decorations and food and fun. It's clear, both families have spent *as much as they could possibly afford* so that this party—and this night—will be remembered forever by the whole town...

And oh! the food looks so delicious to you! You eat your fill of appetizers, main courses, tasty treats and desserts: they have forgotten nothing that you like to eat! And now—*What's that?*—there's music in the air. There's a band of musicians playing—*WOW!*—this is going to be fun!

You head for the dance floor to cut a rug with your friends. And cut a rug you do: all your best moves! At times, the crowd is all circled around you, watching with enormous smiles. And now, here comes the bride and groom too; they're dancing and laughing right alongside you. What a night of celebration this is...

Until, eventually—*Whew!*—you're thirsty from all that dancing...

Leaving the dance floor, you walk across the courtyard to the edge where the wine and water are being served by the helpers; you stand in the open air and watch the joy of the party around you. Overhead, just a sliver of moon is shining clear against the stars; the courtyard is lit by torches and candlelight flickering...

And that's when you can't help noticing a nervous conversation beside you.
Two servants talking in the shadow of a high column.

"There's no more wine," one whispers.

"*What?!*"the other almost shouts. "How can that be?!"

"I don't know," says the first. "I guess they didn't plan on so many coming."

Then, on the other side of you, you hear a different conversation:

"Jesus," a woman says, "there's no more wine."

"So?" the Man responds. "What would you have me do, Mother? My time has not yet come."

But the lady—clearly not listening—walks right past you, says to the helpers, "Do what He says," pointing to her Son, and then heads back out to the dance floor.

All of this has your complete attention now. What will this Man do? What *can* He do?

Here's what He does...

He tells the servants: "Go get those big clay jars—those six over in the corner—and bring them back to Me." They do. They lug them over.

Then He says: "Now fill all six with water, right to the brim—don't leave a drop unfilled." They do. They fill all six to their absolute top.

Then, "Take a cup to the host of the party," the Man says, pointing over. "Let him have a sip. I guarantee he'll like what he tastes."

The helpers aren't sure what to do though. After all, *they've* been working all day long on this party. *They're* the ones who've served the food and drinks; *they're* the ones who noticed the wine running out. What could be worse now than walking a cup of WATER to the host of the party and getting fired from their jobs, right this minute!

But, they do. They walk over. You watch them walk a small clay cup to the host of the party.

And now you're watching him as he takes a sip. You watch as he swirls it around in his mouth for a moment and you see the way his eyes light up!

"The best I've ever tasted!" he shouts. "Where in the world did this delicious wine come from, so late in the party? We should've had this one *first*!"

Amazed, you immediately turn to get another look at the Man who has done this thing, who has made the water wine, who has saved the night, the party, the wedding...

But, amazingly, He's already watching you as you turn to look...

and...

He winks...

before heading back out to dance!

Let's Talk About It

Tell me about the best party you've ever attended. Was there music? Good food? Friends? What do you think made it so fun?

What do you think Jesus loves about parties? What does this show us about His personality?

Chapter 4

The Call on the Water

Luke 5:1-11

Imagine you're sitting on the edge of a boat, with the morning sun on your face, breathing in cool fresh air as you stretch your arms high over your head, yawning. You've only just beached your boat, dragging its bow up the sandy-gravelly shore; now you're sitting and resting from your long night's work. Yes, you've been out there on the deep blue waters of the Sea of Galilee all night, fishing; now it's time to clean the nets and sleep.

Did you have a good night's catch? No. You didn't. Not a single fish is squirming or wiggling in the belly of your boat. Not a one.

So, feeling a little bit frustrated, you spread your net on the golden, sandy-gravelly beach and inspect its joints and ribs for snags and tears. The sun is getting higher over the eastern hills above the lake; the water is sparkling brightly with a million points of its light. As you haul the net back toward yourself and sit down on the edge of your boat to mend it, you are listening to the sounds of the morning. Birds are calling. The marketplace is starting to wake up. Children are on their way to the village school.

But now, even as you've just begun stitching the edge of your net, your ears are starting to notice the sound of a bunch of *different* sounds...

Singing. Laughing. Shouting.

The sound of hundreds, maybe thousands, of people's feet, rising and falling, rising and falling, rising and falling...

You glance at the outer edge of your town—just above the fringe of the harbor shore—and here they come: *unbelievable crowds of people!*

Who are these people? And where have they come from? They are far more than all the people of your town, all put together! And now, here they come. They're walking down toward the very spot you're sitting—down to the edge of the water—and that's when you notice the Man they're following...

He is walking ahead of the crowd, with a spring in His step. The golden light of the morning is upon His face. He seems to be enjoying every moment of this new day, enjoying all the people who are following Him, and, for a moment, you catch *His* eye. He nods His head at you and smiles. You smile back.

At the edge of the water, He suddenly turns on His heel and the whole crowd stops; you hear the crunch of their sandals on the sandy-gravelly beach as they grow quiet. The Man is only a few feet away from you and your boat. He is near enough for you to listen, as He begins speaking:

"The Kingdom of Heaven is like a big net thrown into the sea collecting all kinds of fish. When it is full, the fishermen haul it ashore and sit down and pick out the good ones for the market barrels and—"

But, even as He's saying this, the crowd has continued to inch closer and closer to Him and you watch how He's being pushed back into the sea. He looks at you again. "Mind if I use your boat for a few minutes?" He asks you.

So, next thing you know, you have rowed Him out a few feet and He's sitting in the stern of the boat, back to teaching all the crowds of people again. His voice travels strong and true over the wind-made waves and the people hang on every wonderful word He says.

You are hanging on every wonderful word He says too.

"Have a glorious day!" He says to the crowds, finishing; then He turns on His boat-bench to look at *you*, to talk to *you*.

"So, how was your night of fishing?" He asks.

"*Rotten*," you respond.

He laughs with the most wonderful laugh at the way you said that.

"Well, should we see about fixing that?" He asks, and then points out to sea. "I know of a good spot. Let's go. Just you and me."

And even though you know that this is the *worst* time for fishing—the sun now high over those eastern hills—there is just something about this Man. Something about the way He speaks. The way He looks into your eyes. It's like He already knows everything before it happens...

So, out you row another forty or fifty feet—not too far offshore—and then He says to you, "Here's the spot. Let's fish." And now, together, you and this Man, side by side, are standing up, hauling the net and casting it over the side of the boat into the blue water...

And then...

Something begins to happen.

The whole boat starts to lean and lurch and list and you almost fall right in. *The net is filling full of fish like you've never seen!* You can actually *see* the fish all flopping and flying into the net; it's like they're answering a command: *"Thou shalt get into that net!"* And now the edge of your boat is dropping almost to the waterline; you are beginning to worry that this enormous catch might actually sink your boat!

Which is the exact moment you remember the Man who is next to you. You lift your eyes to see what He is doing right now.

You see that the Man is smiling.

Laughing.

Delighted.

He looks you in the eye.

He says, "From now on, you will fish for *people* instead of fish. Come along now. It's time to follow Me."

You have absolutely no idea what He means or what this *all* might mean. But it just doesn't matter.

You simply *have* to follow this wonderful Man. It's like He has caught your heart forever.

Let's Talk About It

Have you ever tried really hard at something, but it still didn't work out? How did that make you feel?

What do you think it was like for Peter to first meet Jesus and catch all of those fish?

What do you think Jesus meant when He told Peter that he would "fish for people instead of fish"?

Chapter 5

Wonderful Words on a Hillside

Matthew 5, 6 & 7

Imagine sitting amidst the wildflowers of a hillside meadow. Down the sloping grass below you shines the waters of the Sea of Galilee, reflecting all the beauty of the sky overhead. Big, fluffy, bright-white clouds are floating lazily across that beautiful, big blue sky; just the lightest wind is ruffling the surface of the water. In the further distance, the heights of the opposite shoreline show the shadows of those same big clouds; you watch the light and dark pass over them.

It is a perfectly beautiful day, sitting where you're sitting...

Turning back around and looking up now—up the hillside in the direction the crowd around you faces—you are looking right at Jesus. There He is: sitting up above you, on a rock, at the head of the hill, looking back down upon you and the rest of all these people. The same breeze that's blowing over and across the waters, through the grass, through the stalks of the wildflowers, is blowing through His hair...

He raises His hand, suddenly, to speak. Everyone grows quiet, silent, all leaning forward...

"How happy are the humble-hearted, for the kingdom of Heaven is theirs!
"How happy are those who know what sadness is, for they will be given courage and comfort!
"How happy are the gentle, for the whole earth will belong to them!
"How happy are those who are hungry and thirsty for goodness, for they will be fully and
totally satisfied!
"How happy are those with hearts of mercy, for they will have mercy shown to them!
"How happy are the pure in heart, for they will see God!
"How happy are those who make peace, for they will be called sons and daughters of God!
"How happy are those who have suffered all kinds of hardship for the sake of goodness, for
the kingdom of Heaven will belong to them!"

Never once in your life have you ever words like these—words that seem to turn the world upside down... *or is this right side up?* Your heart feels a little bit confused, and yet, also, like these words might be the very words of life. So, again, you focus your mind to listen to Him closely.

He is saying, *"You are the light for the whole world. It is impossible to hide a town built on the top of a hill. And people do not light a lamp and put it under a bucket, do they? No, they put it on a lampstand and it gives its light for everybody in the house to see. So let your light shine like that in the sight of all people. Let them see the good things you do and let them praise your Father in Heaven."*

So far, in all your travels with Jesus, you've been amazed at how He captures your imagination with His beautiful pictures in words. A few moments later, He's doing it all over again:

"I say to you," He says, *"don't you ever worry about living—wondering what you are going to eat or drink, or what you're going to wear. Surely your life is more important than food, and the body more important than the clothes you wear. Look up at the birds in the sky—"*

You look up. Sure enough, a flock of simple starlings are winging their way across the face of the big blue sky, right then...

"These birds never plant seeds or harvest fields or store away in barns, and yet your Heavenly Father feeds them. Aren't you much more valuable to Him than they are?

"And can any of you, however much he worries, make himself an inch taller? And so why do you worry about your clothing? Consider how the wild flowers grow—"

You look around yourself. There they are. Moving gently with the breeze...

"These flowers," He says, "neither work or weave their clothes, but I tell you that even King Solomon in all his glory was never clothed like one of these! And if God so clothes the flowers of the field, which are alive today, and dead and gone tomorrow, is He not very much more likely to clothe you, you people of so little faith?

"So, don't you worry and don't—PLEASE don't!—keep on saying, 'What shall we eat, what shall we drink, what shall we wear?' For that is what the unbelievers are always looking for; your Heavenly Father knows that you need them all, doesn't He? But set your whole entire heart upon the kingdom and His goodness, and all these things will just be given to you."

Yes, that is what I want! you suddenly realize. To have your whole entire heart set upon Jesus! To have a life where you are known by Him, loved by Him, trusting Him to give you all you need, just like He said...

"Everyone then who hears these words of mine and starts to live them is like a wise man who builds his house upon the rock. Down came the rain and up came the floods, while the winds blew and burst against that house—and yet it did not fall because it was built upon the rock.

"Yet everyone who hears these words of mine and does not follow them can be compared to a silly man who built his house upon sand. And down came the rain and up came the floods, while the winds blew and burst against that house till it collapsed, and fell with a great crash."

And, just as suddenly as He'd started all these words, sitting up high in this hillside meadow, He stops; He's done talking. He rises from the rock where He's been sitting and He weaves His way down through the crowds, down in your direction...

And seeing you, He stops; He smiles.

"Want to walk this Way with Me?" He asks.

Let's Talk About It

What surprises you about the people Jesus describes as happy?

What do you think it could look like to hide your light under a basket? Why doesn't Jesus want us to do that?

What are some ways that God has taken care of you? Take some time to list His provision together.

Chapter 6

The Loneliest One Finds Love

Matthew 8:1-4

Imagine not having a single friend in the whole world. Imagine if every time you ever went anywhere or anytime you ever saw anyone, they tried their very best to avoid you.

You see, many years ago, your life changed forever. One morning, you woke up to your day, got out of bed, started getting dressed, and, looking down, you noticed you couldn't quite feel the feeling of your hands. And, with that, you noticed some strange-looking marks and markings on your skin—*that wasn't there a week ago!*—and yet you didn't give it another thought till that afternoon. That was because, while you were walking down through the marketplace that afternoon, someone suddenly shouted:

"Leper! Leper! Get away, leper!"

You looked all around to see which person had leprosy—who was the one whose life would be ruined—and then you realized...

It was you.

The crowd in the busy market was all looking at *you*. *Yours* was the life that now, was forever ruined.

You see, everyone in your town and in this countryside believed that this disease called leprosy could only be passed along by being near it. They thought that if they ever touched a person with your condition, they would also become a "leper," a person with leprosy. So, ever since that afternoon in the market, you have lived your life at the edge of people, far away from your former friends. You live in a tiny shack on the ridge of a hill. You only get your food by people leaving it, down below. You get your water by walking down the valley to a brook. No one ever comes to see you anymore.

And, as if all that loneliness and sadness and solitude weren't bad enough, your disease has only gotten worse. What had started with that little patch of redness on your hand has slowly crept across the entirety of your body. Sometimes, when you lean to get a drink of water at the brook, you catch a glimpse of your reflection in the water there. You don't even look like yourself anymore. Your face looks almost scary with the disease's spread. With blotches, splotches, and growths, your skin tight and reddened, sometimes all you want to do is sit down and cry.

That is, until... today.

Today, sitting on the doorstep of your house, you started noticing crowds of people walking up the hillside, two hills over. They were walking in great big groups—first, dozens; then, hundreds; eventually, thousands of people, all climbing up the grassy hillside. Then they disappeared behind the edge of the nearer hill and you imagined they had stopped in a particular grassy, flowery meadow. You have often walked, alone, through that meadow and so you decide to sneak a bit closer, to see where all the crowds are going...

A few minutes later, you are lying at the edge of that meadow, and you are listening to the most wonderful words, while hiding in the tall grass. To the end of your days, you will never forget those words:

"So, don't you worry and don't—PLEASE don't!—keep on saying, 'What shall we eat, what shall we drink, what shall we wear?' For that is what the unbelievers are always looking for; your Heavenly Father knows that you need them all, doesn't He?

"But set your whole entire heart upon the kingdom and His goodness, and all these things will just be given to you."

The Speaker of these words is sitting high up on the hillside, on a rock, with the glowing sun upon His face. Through the grass, you are watching Him as He speaks and, suddenly, something in your heart says, "He will help you. This is the Man who will set you free."

But you also know that walking into that crowd, mixing with people, seeing the villagers, is a thing that can never be forgiven by them. You still remember how it felt when that first person shouted, "Leper! Leper!" and you're terrified of living through that embarrassment again.

Yet, again, you watch the Man at the head of the meadow; how He speaks these words of life so lovingly, so true-heartedly. And now you're standing to your feet and you are walking down the edge of the hill—into the meadow—as you watch that Man descending. You can see how people jump away, run away, from the moment they first see you… but you simply don't care anymore. You must get near to that Teacher, right now. That is the only thought running through your head.

And finally… here He is.

He's just a few feet off, now. You sink down on your knees, kneeling amidst the flowers and the grass, and you hold your hands out to Him. "Lord," you say, "if you are willing to, I believe you can make me clean."

The Man stops walking; He stands still. The whole crowd quiets down to a hush. The Man's head turns a little to one side—He is watching you, observing you—and then He takes a step closer.

He is reaching out to touch you with His hand!

You haven't felt a single touch in many years; you are almost afraid as He leans closer, closer, closer. Yet here He comes, reaching down, reaching out, and, suddenly, you feel the most amazing feeling you've ever felt. The Teacher has taken ahold of your arm and a glorious feeling of warmth—almost like a shock—is bridging away from His hand. You feel that warmth as it spreads out, spreading up, all throughout your body, and then He says to you:

"Of course I want to! Be clean!"

And it's when you hear the gasping of the crowd that you suddenly realize you've been closing your eyes—you open them—*you can't believe what your eyes see…*

A hand that looks just like it did before. An arm that's smooth, like a baby's skin.

You run your fingers over your face and you can tell that it's just like it used to be, back before this all started…

For a moment, you are trying to figure out what one should say to such a Healer who has forever set you free from a life like death.

But He speaks to *you* before you even have a chance to thank Him:

"Follow Me," He says, and smiles.

69

Let's Talk About It

Can you think of anyone who other kids tease or don't want to play with? Have you ever experienced being left out or avoided? What was that like?

What are some of the ways Jesus communicated His love for the leper in the story?

Chapter 7

Through the Roof

Matthew 9:1-8, Mark 2:1-12, Luke 5:17-26

Imagine sitting on the dusty, rough wooden floor of a simple little house—a house *absolutely packed* from wall to wall with people. There are people sitting on the floor just like you are. There are people sitting on chairs and stools they have dragged here from their homes. There are people standing and blocking the view; there are people sitting up on the windowsills; there are even others who lean through those windows, trying to hear.

You are sitting in this simple little house, crowded with all these people, because, at the center of the room, sits Jesus from Nazareth.

He is sitting in a chair, His legs comfortably crossed, smiling His friendly smile, and, like so often, He is in the middle of the most wonderful story. It is a story about how faith in God is just like a seed and how, if you plant it, it will grow and grow and grow. It's just the most marvelous picture for how you want to live your life and how—

What was that?

Something just fell on the top of your head!

Reaching up, you brush your hair with your hand and a whole mess of dust and straw comes whisking past your nose. It's on your shoulders too.

Where did that dust just drop from? you wonder.

You try to focus on Jesus again.

He is talking about that seed of faith and the soil and the rain falling down to water it, and you're almost back to focusing...

Suddenly, *a piece of the ceiling falls down in front of you!*

People jump to their feet and try to get away; there's even a man who was knocked to the floor by that mess that just fell down! The poor guy looks like He was caught up in a dust storm: He is coated from head to foot in bits of plaster, and sticks, and straw, and dust, and dirt...

He wipes His eyes with the tips of His fingers. He grins.

You realize the Man is Jesus!

And now, with Him, you are looking up at the ceiling, at the rafters, at the *hole that's starting to open up above!* You can't believe it. There are hammers and hands and chisels and fingers digging and clawing and scraping the roof from the topside, coming in! The entire crowd of people inside is looking up now...

The hole above grows bigger and bigger...until...

The hole is just as big as a man!

Then, next thing you know, the group of men on the roof are peering in, looking down through the hole, and they're scanning the crowd looking for something. Seeing Jesus, they light up. They have been tearing a hole in the roof in order to see Jesus.

And then, for a second, they disappear...

The whole crowd waits, wondering...

And now, they are dragging a man on a stretcher toward the hole in the roof and, taking up ropes, they're lowering him right into the room! He glides down into the middle of all the people and all the people are trying to back away and give him a place to land. And, sure enough—BUMP—he lands right in front of Jesus...

Everyone is holding their breath...

What will Jesus say or do? Or do or say?

Will He shout up through the roof about the damage; will He scold the man before Him; will He ask for His cloak to be dry-cleaned?

What will Jesus do?

Well, Jesus smiles. Then He laughs. Then He shakes His head. "My friend" He says to the man lying before Him on the floor, "your sins are forgiven!"

There is instantly a murmuring over your shoulder. You look back. There is a row of religious leaders behind you. They are whispering to each other: *Who is this man who acts like He's God? Only God can forgive sins—not men!*

And now you're turning back toward Jesus to see what will happen. He's looking right back past you at those very religious leaders. "Why are you thinking those thoughts in your hearts?" He asks them. "Which do you think is easier to say: 'Your sins are forgiven' or 'Get up and walk'?"

Then Jesus rises to His feet above the man who lies on the stretcher, smiles at him, and then He looks back at the religious leaders. "But," He says, "so that you may understand that I have the power to forgive sins, I'll do this..."

He looks down at the man. "I tell you," He says, "Get up... walk... and go home."

And the man on the floor—a man you're starting to recognize as that paralyzed beggar from downtown—sits up. He leans forward. His eyes have filled with a strange sort of joy that you have never seen on the face of a man—*ever*—in your whole life. Because...

he is rising to his feet!

He picks up the cloth-covered bed on which he'd been lying and, lightly whistling to himself, walks his way right out of the room! The man who'd never ever walked before is *strutting!* You watch him disappear out into the street...

And looking back at Jesus, wondering what He will say or do—or do or say—next, you see that His eyes are looking over your shoulder again.

He is watching the religious leaders silently leaving the house.

He is watching the way they're whispering to each other.

Let's Talk About It

Why do you think the paralyzed man's friends cut a hole in the roof?

Talk about a time when your friends helped you to do something that you couldn't do on your own.

Why do you think the religious leaders acted like that at the end of the story?

Chapter 8

The Storm & the Hush

Matthew 8:23-27, Mark 4:35-41, Luke 8:22-25

Imagine the peaceful sounds of a boat sailing quiet waters. The almost silence of the hull cutting through the seas. The gentle whisper of the wind coming up behind, filling the sail. The rippling sound of the sail as it tightens and tugs. The calming creak of the ropes pulling against the mast. The distant call of a bird winging its way through the darkness.

Now, imagine how you'd feel as you rested your back against the rim of the boat, listening to these sounds, watching the gray clouds against the night sky. How wonderfully restful and relaxed you'd be feeling. How you might turn to a friend and strike up a nice, nighttime conversation. How you'd stretch your legs in front of you, feeling sleepy, feeling content, feeling the warm west wind as it played across your face...

Well, that was all twenty minutes ago.

All that peace and rest is over now.

Now, an unbelievable storm has descended off the hills, with wind rushing from the heights, and the water around you boiling and pitching and troughing and smashing. Where before the sounds were silence, whispers, ripplings, creakings, and calls, now the night is full of SHOUTING, SCREAMING, TEARING, CRASHING, and FEAR. Now your boat is tumbling down a wave's face into a pit of dark water; in the next moment, you are rising, rising, rising up another. The waters are coming over both sides of the boat—you see your friends bailing it out with buckets— and you're starting to hear a scary sound that sounds like the mast beginning to splinter and break. All at once, lightning suddenly flashes. For just that split second, you can clearly see all the chaos around you.

What will you do? What *can* you do?

And that's when you remember that Jesus is in the stern—there in the back of the boat—and you wonder what He's been doing during all of this? Finding your balance, you hold the edge of the boat and walk back, stepping over the seats and tackle, and you're hoping He hasn't been thrown overboard...

And there He is: asleep.

ASLEEP!

He is lying on a comfortable cushion, asleep, despite all the wind and the waves. There's the slightest hint of a smile on His lips—perhaps He's dreaming—and you almost feel sorry as you grab His shoulder to shake Him awake.

He makes that funny face He always makes when waking. Blinks His eyes a few times, trying to get His bearings. Then He yawns. Stretches His arms high over His head and sits up. And now He's looking at you, like, "What? What's the meaning of this midnight wake-up?"

"JESUS," you shout, "DON'T YOU CARE THAT WE MIGHT DROWN?"

He doesn't say a word in response to your question.

Instead, He stands up to His feet, puts His hands on His hips, and stares out into the wind and waves and lightning and sprays and darkness.

"Hush," He whispers under His breath. All He does is whisper that one word.

And if you hadn't been there, hadn't seen what happened next, hadn't *experienced* the whole thing for yourself, you'd never in a million years believe what your own eyes now see for themselves.

Glassy waters.

The drip-drip of droplets falling from the sailcloth.

The absolute silence of a slack wind.

The twinkling of a million-billion stars in a clear sky.

Looking at Jesus, you watch Him as He turns around, sits back down on His comfortable cushion in the stern, and smiles with that funny half-smile of His.

"Why were you so frightened?" He asks you. "What has happened to your trust in Me?"

And that's the very first moment—the moment He settles Himself back down to sleep the rest of the night on His comfortable cushion—that you realize that Jesus created EVERYTHING.

That the whole entire world came from His command.

From His Word.

Including you.

That's what you're thinking about as you fall asleep on the calm waters.

Let's Talk About It

Have you ever felt as scared as the disciples in the storm? What made you afraid?

Picture that scary moment in your imagination, but this time picture Jesus there with you. Is He scared? What is He doing? What is He saying? How do you feel about that situation now that He's there with you?

Chapter 9

Sharing a Meal with Jesus

Matthew 14:13-21, Mark 6:30-44, Luke 9:10-17, John 6:1-14

Imagine the rumbly feeling of your stomach when you've been waiting to eat a meal, far past the point when you were *already* really hungry. In fact, you were already totally famished about four hours ago—OH, SO HUNGRY!—but you're in a big group and didn't want to be impolite by breaking out your food. Plus, you noticed, it didn't seem like anyone else's mom or dad had remembered to bring a single bite to eat. But—GOODNESS GRACIOUS!—you are tummy-rumbling hungry, famished, impatient, tired, and getting a little ready to shout out: "Snack break!"

You are sitting in a vast, open, seaside meadow. It is late afternoon; a half-cloudy sky is overhead. The autumn light is starting to cast long shadows over and across the meadow; the golden light of the soon-to-be sunset is against your face. Trying to stop your hunger from making you angry, you start to watch the movement of the grass with the breeze right in front of you. It swirls and whirls and dances and does a little bow away from the wind. You start to imagine the grass is onstage, like a dancer...

And that's when you begin to notice the murmuring of the people, that the Teacher has stopped teaching, and that His friends, His disciples, are walking through the crowd. They are walking amidst families and groups and groupings who've come from villages together and they're asking: "Does anyone have any food?"

Apparently, no one has any food.

And if you hadn't been sitting and listening to the wonderful words of Jesus all afternoon, you might not have said a word about the picnic basket you've been sitting on...

But *because* you've been sitting and listening to the wonderful words of Jesus, you suddenly hear yourself piping up: "Right here! I've got some!"

And now, holding the hand of a friend of Jesus—his name is Andrew, you found out—you are approaching the front of the crowd to actually meet Jesus for yourself!

Jesus!

The Man from Nazareth!

That miracle-making Carpenter-Teacher who's taken Galilee by storm: you are just about to meet Him in the flesh!

And it's everything you ever hoped it would be.

With a kindly smile, He kneels down on one knee and shakes your hand; He is treating you like the much more grown-up person you know yourself to be. And with a hearty thanks, He accepts your basket of food—five loaves and two fish—and now He's standing up, turning back to His friends.

You begin to watch Him very closely now. You have a sense that something fantastic is about to happen right in front of you.

And here's what it looks like:

He lifts His hands to Heaven and, with a smile, begins to thank His Heavenly Father for His "new friend" who'd been so kind in giving up his lunch. (This is YOU, you suddenly realize!) And now, starting to break the bread and gently tearing at a portion of the first fish, He gives a handful of each to the first of His disciples. Then to the second. Then to the third...

And now you're watching how these Twelve are taking baskets full of food to each of the groups who are sitting nearest the spot where Jesus stands. Then they go farther back. Then, even farther back. You watch how the people nearer are then asking for seconds and thirds; and you watch—*amazed*—as those people are actually *getting* seconds and thirds!

And that's when you begin watching Jesus again.

Time and again, He is breaking bread, tearing fish, handing out; then He's reaching over to grab more and more and more to share. What had been the meal your mother packed you this morning is now spread out across the endless fields of people, eating in the evening air.

And that's the exact moment you finally let your mind and heart understand the immensity of the miracle that Jesus is doing right in front of you. You realize you've never ever seen a crowd this big in your life—five, eight, ten, or twelve thousand?—and now *they're all eating your lunch!*

And how does this amazing day end for you?

Well, what do you expect?

You see, once He's finished feeding the entirety of the crowd, Jesus then turns to *you*, saying: "And how about you and I have *our* meal together?"

You have a perfectly wonderful dinner with Jesus, sitting in the grass. He lets you ask a million questions about a million things. He's all the more interesting when you catch Him for a quiet minute by yourself, like this.

Just wait till you tell your mom!

Let's Talk About It

Imagine yourself in this scenario. What would have made it hard for you to share your lunch with Jesus and the crowds?

Talk about the last time you shared something with someone else. Ask Jesus if there is anything He'd like for you to share with somebody today!

Chapter 10

Nothing to Be Afraid Of

Matthew 14:22-33, Mark 6:45-52, John 6:16-21

Imagine you're sitting in a boat with all your best friends around you. You're in the middle of an enormous lake, surrounded by rolling hills. It is nighttime. The red and golden sunset faded away from the western sky an hour or two ago. All evening the wind has been blowing gently from the northwest; your boat's sail has been full and puffing out nicely. You and your friends have been talking, telling stories, laughing at a joke from the day before; but now you're all tired, getting quieter and quieter...

Suddenly, a hard wind comes from another direction. You look up. Your sailboat's sail is flapping wildly, dancing back and forth against the dark night sky. You can hear the jangling of the ropes and riggings against the mast and the ties; some of your fishermen friends look worried. *Something is up!* Quietly, they all move forward, lower the sail, hand around oars, and seem to be preparing for the whole night to change.

Before you know it, the whole night *has* changed. Winds from every direction. The water swirling and whirling; waves starting to build and crash. And next thing you know, you are feeling the bottom of the boat beginning to fill with water: it rises above your ankles, the waves are coming over the side of the boat!

So you are grabbing a bucket, filling it up, bailing the water out of the boat, back into the sea, and yet the sea keeps spitting it back in! You start to have a feeling in your belly that this night isn't going to end well. You begin to wish *so much* that you hadn't left Jesus back on shore...

You know, if He was here, it'd be just fine. It'd be just like that *other* night with the storm on the sea. If only Jesus was here, asleep in the stern, you'd walk right back to Him, wake Him up, and He'd hush the storm, just like before. If only Jesus was here with you...

And that's when you happen to look up for a moment. Perhaps something caught the corner of your eye. *What is that little speck of white in the far distance?* you wonder to yourself.

But then you're filling your bucket, throwing out the water, hearing your friends' shouts and screams and questions and fears: *Oh, you are so frightened!*

Until you glance back out in the direction of that shape on the water.
Now it seems to be getting bigger, nearer...

But then you're back, again, to more of your bucketing and bailing, with the wind and water and darkness all around you, the sound of the night overpowering your senses.

And then you look up one more time.

There He is.

Jesus.

Standing out there on the surface of the dark waters.

He rolls and dips with the rolling and dipping of the waves and yet, there He is, on the water, just a few feet from the edge of the boat...

"It's me," He says, looking you directly in the eye. "No need to be afraid anymore."

You are no longer afraid at all. How can anyone be afraid when they know this Jesus? Whether He's sleeping in the stern and bringing His "Hush!" to the storm, or whether He's walking on the water, He always does it: He always arrives.

Jesus will never stop arriving for you, you realize.

From the water, He asks you if you'd like to come and walk with Him: to try the experience of walking on water with Him?

Will you say yes?

Tonight, will you step over the edge of the boat?

Let's Talk About It

What makes you feel better when you're afraid?

Imagine that Jesus is right beside you the next time you feel scared
What would trusting Him look like for you?

Chapter 11

Jesus as He Really Is

Matthew 17:1-9, Mark 9:2-8, Luke 9:28-36, 2 Peter 1:16-18

Imagine you're taking a hike, high above the waters of the Galilee, following a narrow trail through bends and turns and twists and rises. You are climbing amidst the tall, rugged rocks of a mountainside, following after Jesus as He climbs higher and higher. He had turned to you and two of the others earlier today and invited you "up" with Him— "up" to *where* you didn't get the chance to ask. And, ever since, you have been silently following after Him: struggling and straining as He climbs higher and higher up this narrow trail.

Where in the world are we going? you wonder to yourself. The late-day sun feels hot upon your face. You occasionally turn around and look back down the trail toward the Sea of Galilee, wishing you were swimming in its blue waters...

But, higher, higher, higher, Jesus hikes up. Will He never, ever stop?

Well, suddenly, He stops. He motions the three of you to sit down under the shade of a tree. You have arrived in an open stretch of level ground, rounded about by tall, reddish boulders, like walls around you. Sitting down in the shade of that one little tree, you suddenly realize just how tired this day of hiking has made you. All the twisting and turning, hiking up, hiking down, climbing, climbing, climbing, climbing has got you feeling like you could take a nap.

For a moment, you are trying to fight it...

Then...

you're not...

Because now you're asleep.

And it's when you start to feel yourself awaking that you suddenly realize the whole world around you is flooded with light. But it's more than light; the feeling against your face and the front of your eyelids is far more powerful—you're almost afraid to open up your eyes.

But, finally, you open them. Just a little. You try to just peer out and see whatever there is to see. You only barely open your eyes and yet—*immediately!*—you are overwhelmed by exactly what it is you're seeing.

Jesus… but Jesus with a face like the sun.

Jesus glowing gloriously, like every ounce of all the light and glory in the universe got together and descended upon Him all at once. And there's two other men, glowing there beside Him.

One is saying to Jesus, "You, Jesus, are the One the Lord our God has raised up, a prophet like me, from among the people! Our Father God has put His words in your mouth, and you speak to all the people all that our Father God commands!"

You know those words: this man must be mighty Moses!

Now the other man is saying, "You, Jesus, are the fire of Heaven falling upon the earth; you are also the sacrifice consumed."

And you remember the story of that sacrifice and fire from the writings of the prophets: this other man must be the prophet Elijah!

And that's the exact moment that Peter opens his big mouth!

"Master," he says, "it is wonderful that we should get to be here with you! Let me put up a tent… or a house… or a shack, so that you and Moses and Elijah have a place to stay—"

But even before those words have left his lips, a thunderous sound from Heaven shakes the whole earth beneath you:

"THIS IS MY SON, MY CHOSEN! LISTEN TO HIM!"

As you feel the ground you're lying on finally stop shaking from that voice, you almost feel brave enough to look up. You have no idea if the sky and the mountains and the tree will even be there anymore: so powerful was the booming of that voice from Heaven.

So, you prepare yourself to open your eyes, to look up…

You are telling yourself, *Be strong, be courageous…*

When you finally open your eyes and turn your gaze toward that scene from just before...

Only Jesus is standing there.

He is standing in the middle of the level ground, totally alone, totally Himself, with just His normal cloak, sandals, and that look on His face. He is quietly regarding you, Peter and John, as the three of you are huddled under the shade of that little sapling.

"Have you begun to begin to understand who I AM?" He asks.

"Yes," you say, *"I have begun to begin."*

Let's Talk About It

Draw a picture or describe what you think Jesus looks like in His
heavenly form.

How would you feel if you suddenly saw Him like that?

Chapter 12

The Resurrection & the Life

John 11:1-44

Imagine that you are crying. Really crying. Your shoulders shake as you sob uncontrollably. You have been crying most of the day already, and there's nothing anyone can do to stop you from crying for the rest of it. You can feel how sadness wells up from your belly into your heart and mind, like a wave building and cresting and crashing. Over and over, the memory of loss and grief comes back to you; you are struck again by what you've lost. *Oh, you sob and sob!*

You just keep thinking of your dear, wonderful brother. He died just four days before this...

You start to rise to your feet to find another handkerchief; suddenly, surprisingly, you're completely caught off guard. Your eyes look out the open door, up the road. You see a woman walking down toward the house—it's your sister—and you're surprised at the look on her face.

Happy. Laughing. Joyful.

Like the last four days had never happened.

And in she walks and up she comes directly to you and she is saying, "Mary, the Master's here and is asking for you."

And you can hardly believe the complete and utter change that's suddenly comes over your heart:

Happy. Laughing. Joyful.

Like the last four days had never happened.

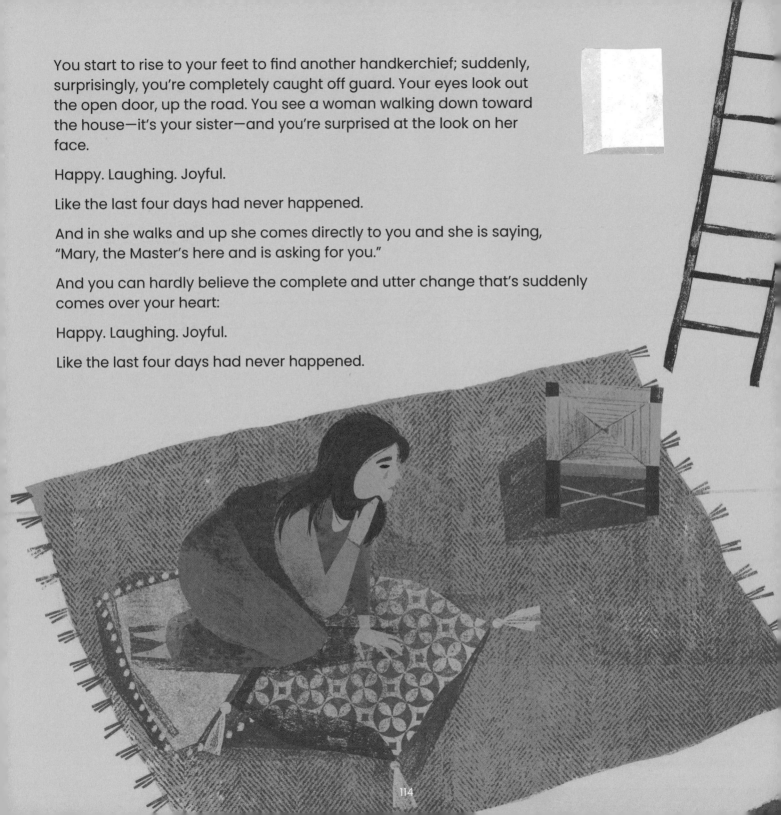

You jump into your shoes and run right out the door and down the street; it's almost impossible for you to run any faster! You are twisting and turning down and around the web of streets, out toward the edge of town, and then, suddenly, you stop. You are staring at a Man standing on the horizon. He gently waves and you run to Him.

Falling on your knees before this Man, you start to cry again, saying: "If only you had been here, Lord! If you had been here, I know that my brother wouldn't have died—"

"Where have you put him, Mary?" the Man asks you.

"Lord, come and I will show you," you reply.

But even before you can rise again to go, rise to start the walk to show Him the tomb, you can hear the sound of Jesus crying. Really crying. His shoulders shake as He sobs uncontrollably. You can see how sadness wells up from His belly into His heart and mind, like a wave building and cresting and crashing. Over and over, the reality of loss and grief comes back; He is struck again by what He's lost. *Oh, He sobs and sobs!*

Jesus weeps just like you did before...

Within a few minutes, you, your sister, Martha, and a crowd of your friends are standing outside the tomb. You are standing right outside this cave in the hillside where, inside, lies the body of your dear brother. His name was Lazarus. He was the closest friend you could ever imagine...

And right in front of you—between you and your friends, and the stone in front of the tomb— stands this Man who, moments before, was weeping at His loss. He is not weeping anymore now. He is simply staring at that stone covering the tomb.

"Take away the stone," He says, suddenly.

Your friends mumble and murmur: *How inappropriate!*

Then Martha quietly says, "But Lord, he has been inside for four days already. There will probably already be a smell..."

Jesus turns to look at Martha. It's like there's lightning in His eyes!

"Didn't I tell you," He says, "that if you believed in Me, you would clearly see the wonders God can do?"

So, Martha motions for the stone to be rolled away. A number of workmen begin the enormous task. They struggle and strain to slowly roll the stone aside; it rumbles and grumbles and, finally, stops beside the now-open tomb...

Jesus is looking up toward the heavens.

"Father," He says, "I thank You that You have heard Me. And I know that You're always hearing Me. But I'm saying this now so that these friends will believe and will believe that You have sent Me."

Then He looks right at the open mouth of the tomb. He takes a step closer and then shouts loudly:

"LAZARUS! LAZARUS, COME OUT!"

To you, it feels like *just forever* passes, standing there in the hot afternoon sun, watching the opening of this burial cave in the hillside. As the seconds tick away, you are looking over at Martha, wondering what in the world she is thinking right now. You are beginning to think about your loss again, of how life will be without your brother being around anymore. You are starting to think of how you will feel, in a week, in a month, when—

What?! What is that sound?

Listen!

What is that sound like something bouncing—*BUMP, BUMP, BUMP, BUMP*—that seems to be coming from inside the tomb?

And, even before you have the opportunity to take a step closer, to look for yourself, it is already happening...

A body, wrapped in strips of burial cloths, is hop-hop-hopping its way out of the tomb, into the afternoon light!

Your brother! Lazarus!

Alive!

"Unbind him," Jesus says to all of you. "It's time for him to go home now."

And now you turn directly to Jesus, to Martha, and He puts His hands upon your shoulders, and says, "See? Didn't I tell you that I am the Resurrection and the Life? The one who believes in Me will never die at all."

You turn around, again, to look at your brother. They've just unbound his smiling, surprised face…

And now you look again at Jesus. This friend of yours who *is* the Resurrection and the Life.

Let's Talk About It

Why do you think Jesus cried? How do you think Mary felt to see Jesus cry for her brother like that?

What did Jesus teach people about Father God when He raised Lazarus from the dead?

Chapter 13

The Entry of a King

Matthew 21:1-11, Mark 11:1-11, Luke 19:28-40, John 12:12-19

Imagine the sort of day when you *think* you already know everything that's bound to happen: all the people you'll see, the things you'll do, the way it'll end. You roll out of bed and *think* you already understand everything there is to know, that nothing can surprise you in the way this day might go. So, on *that* sort of day, you've been doing the things you planned to do all morning; then, in the early afternoon, you're on the way to do some other things. Nothing in this day is *too* exciting, *too* boring, *too* attention grabbing; it is a very normal sort of day for you.

Until...

suddenly...

it's not.

126

You are coming along the upper end of the market street, where it bends a little and then jogs a bit, and you're looking up toward the Mount of Olives. Its greenish color looks lovely against the deep blue sky. And now you've turned along an alleyway that cuts between a row of buildings—shadowy and cool...

And that's the moment the day changes entirely.

You see, coming out of the shaded half-darkness of the alley, your eyes are all lit up by the brightness of the sunlight, out in the open. It takes a moment for your eyes to adjust to all that light. And, as they do, you suddenly realize that around you stands a crowd of many thousands of people, all looking up toward the Mount. They are acting very strangely, too, all these people. They have taken off their outer cloaks—some of them very expensive—and they've thrown them down on the roadway in front of you. Others are coming down from the hills with their hands full of grass and grain to cover up the edges of the street's cobbles. And you start to notice others who have sawed off all the branches of the palm trees and they're starting now to wave them.

Wave them for *what*? you wonder.

You don't have to wonder very long.

For, up the street, coming down the hillside into the city, down from the Mount of Olives, there is a Man riding on a donkey. At first, He is too far away to see anything particularly interesting about Him, so you, instead, watch the people all around you. They are crying, laughing, singing, shouting, yelling. You have never seen the people of Jerusalem act like this. Then, together, like a choir, they begin to chant and shout and sing together these words:

"God bless the King who comes in the name of the Lord!
There is now peace in Heaven and glory on high!"

Over and over and over, they sing and shout these words...

When the Man finally rides by the spot where you're standing, you are studying Him: you try to understand why the crowd has gone so wild. Why do these people think this Man is a king; why do they wave the palms and drop their coats in the dirty roadway?

But nothing you see answers these questions...

He seems to you just like any other man...

And you are just about to turn and leave...

when He suddenly turns His head.

For a moment, He is looking in your direction—right in the middle of the crowd—and this "King who comes in the name of the Lord" is watching *you*. He is watching your face and your eyes and your expression to understand what *you* are feeling; whether *you* believe He is King of Kings.

And then He's past; He has passed along your stretch of road and He's riding atop His donkey in the direction of the city center...

But, then, one more time, He turns atop the donkey...

searches for you...

and your eyes meet.

In less than a week, this Man will be killed by this crowd. And you'll never forget that look in His eyes.

Let's Talk About It

Why did people crowd in the streets to see Jesus?

What do you think He was feeling and thinking about as He looked into your eyes at the end of the story?

Chapter 14

A Servant Only

John 13:1-17

Imagine walking up a flight of narrow stairs lit by candlelight, at the top of which is a door that leads to a warm, comfortable room. You know that in that room are all your friends—and a meal—and Jesus; you walk up the stairs with excitement to see everyone inside. The gentle light of the candle glimmers and dances along the staircase.

You are almost there...

Last couple steps...

When you reach the top, you walk in through the doorway. In the room is a long, plain, rough wooden table that takes up most of the room, with more candles atop it. Their faint glow lights the faces of your eleven best friends— and the food on the table—and then, there He is, Jesus. He is sitting at the head of the table, waiting for you.

Quietly, you sit down in the last empty seat. On the table before you, the Passover feast is already laid and ready: unleavened bread, the lamb's meat, the special cups of wine. You can remember the last two years of sharing Passover with Jesus and your friends; this is a special tradition that already means so much to you...

And you're beginning to think of last year's Passover when you notice that Jesus has risen, walked across the room, taken off His coat and tunic, and hung them up. Then He crosses across the room again—to the other corner— and He leans down into the darkness to pick up a bowl. A large clay bowl.

He pours some water into the bowl, using the bowl and jug that are meant for the servants to come and wash the guests' feet—

What is Jesus doing? you wonder to yourself. Those servants will be along any minute. There is no reason for Jesus to take the time to get this bowl and water ready when, obviously, that is another person's job...

That is the work of a servant only.

Yet now you watch as Jesus walks across the middle of the room—His movements lit by candle flames dancing—and gets down upon His knees. He kneels at the feet of your friend, John, and now He takes off John's sandals and He's setting them to the side. And now, with tender, graceful, gentle hands, He holds John's foot over the bowl: *He is washing your friend John's dirty foot!* He soaks up water from the bowl and runs the wet towel against the full length of John's foot. He takes His time. Every inch of both of John's feet receives the same careful attention and service. Then, finishing, He leans a little forward to dab John's feet with the dry towel He'd hung around His waist.

The whole room is silent: shocked. The only sound is the creaking of the floorboards under Jesus.

And that's when you realize He is looking over at you, that you will be the next to receive this footwashing. Your stomach ties in knots: it doesn't seem proper, or right, for the Teacher to be doing this sort of thing for His disciple.

"No, Lord!" you say, suddenly. "You must never wash *my* feet!"

He regards you, with His head turned a little on one side.

"But," He says, "if I do not wash you, you really won't be a part of me. And of what I've come to do."

What can you say to that?

So here He comes. He carries over the bowl and towel, kneels before your feet: Jesus is going to wash *your* feet. You feel the way He takes off each of your sandals and how He lovingly, gently, tenderly takes your feet, one at a time, in hand. As He does this, you are looking down at the bowed-down head of Jesus underneath you; you watch Him with complete fascination. The top of His long dark hair is visible in the golden candlelight; His face is hidden as He finishes what He's doing for you.

Then, for a moment, He looks up at you.

He smiles.

His love overwhelms every part of your heart.

And you remember a particular afternoon—and suddenly it all makes sense to you—when He said, "The Son of Man did not come to *be* served, but to serve…"

You will always remember the night Jesus washed your feet.

This is what He came to do.

Let's Talk About It

If you could have dinner with Jesus, what would you want to eat together? What questions would you ask Him?

Why did Jesus wash the disciples' dirty feet?

How do you feel when you get to help someone else? Think of one thing you could do today to serve someone!

Chapter 15

He Knows What He's Doing

Matthew 26:36-27:31, Mark 14:32-15:20, Luke 22:39-23:25, John 18:1-19:17

Imagine the greatest feeling of fear you could ever feel. Your stomach starts to twist; your throat feels like it wants to choke you; your skin is suddenly cool and crawling like a spider is walking it. Your heart has dropped all the way down to your feet. You have never been scared in your life like you're scared right now.

Only a few minutes ago, you and Jesus and all your friends were up in that peaceful garden on the edge of the Mount of Olives. The quiet moonlight was shining through the olive tree branches. Jesus was off in the distance, praying. But then, suddenly, He stood up straight and walked right past each one of you and into the darkness that looked back down the mountainside. You could tell He was watching something down below. You walked over to His side to see for yourself.

You could see a long line of torches coming up the trail. Like a slithering snake of firelight in the darkness.

And then you were beginning to hear something: Armor. Swords. Shields. Rattling and clanging.

Within moments, a group of soldiers sent from the high priest arrived to the calm and quiet darkness of the garden. Jesus went right out toward them.

"Who are you looking for?" He asked.

"Jesus of Nazareth," they replied, toughly, roughly.

"I am He," He said to them, quietly, gently.

And yet, as if a mighty wave—or a hurricane wind—had suddenly bowled them over, all those soldiers were thrown to the ground at His voice. Jesus stood right there before them, and asked again:

"Who was it you said you were looking for?"

"Jesus of Nazareth," they said, but afraid this time.

"And I tell you again, I am He," Jesus said.

And as He let those men arrest Him, bind His hands with chains, and lead Him off into the darkness, He cast a look in your direction. And in His eyes you saw peace—and joy.

It was clear He knew what He was doing...

And so, now, as you've wandered down the hillside, creeping after Jesus and the soldiers, you have arrived at the high priest's palace. Its high stone walls rise like a fortress; you were fortunate enough to slip through the gate into its inner courtyard. And you've been watching, up above, where Jesus stands before the high priest and the other religious rulers in a half-dark room. You can't hear their words from down where you're standing, but you can certainly tell those men are filled with hatred by the way they shout. Over and over again, they shout in His face. One of them even steps forward and slaps Him.

And as you're watching those men confront Him, shout at Him, slap His face, cover Him with abuse, He looks down at you. In His eyes you see the same peace and joy.

It's still clear He knows what He is doing...

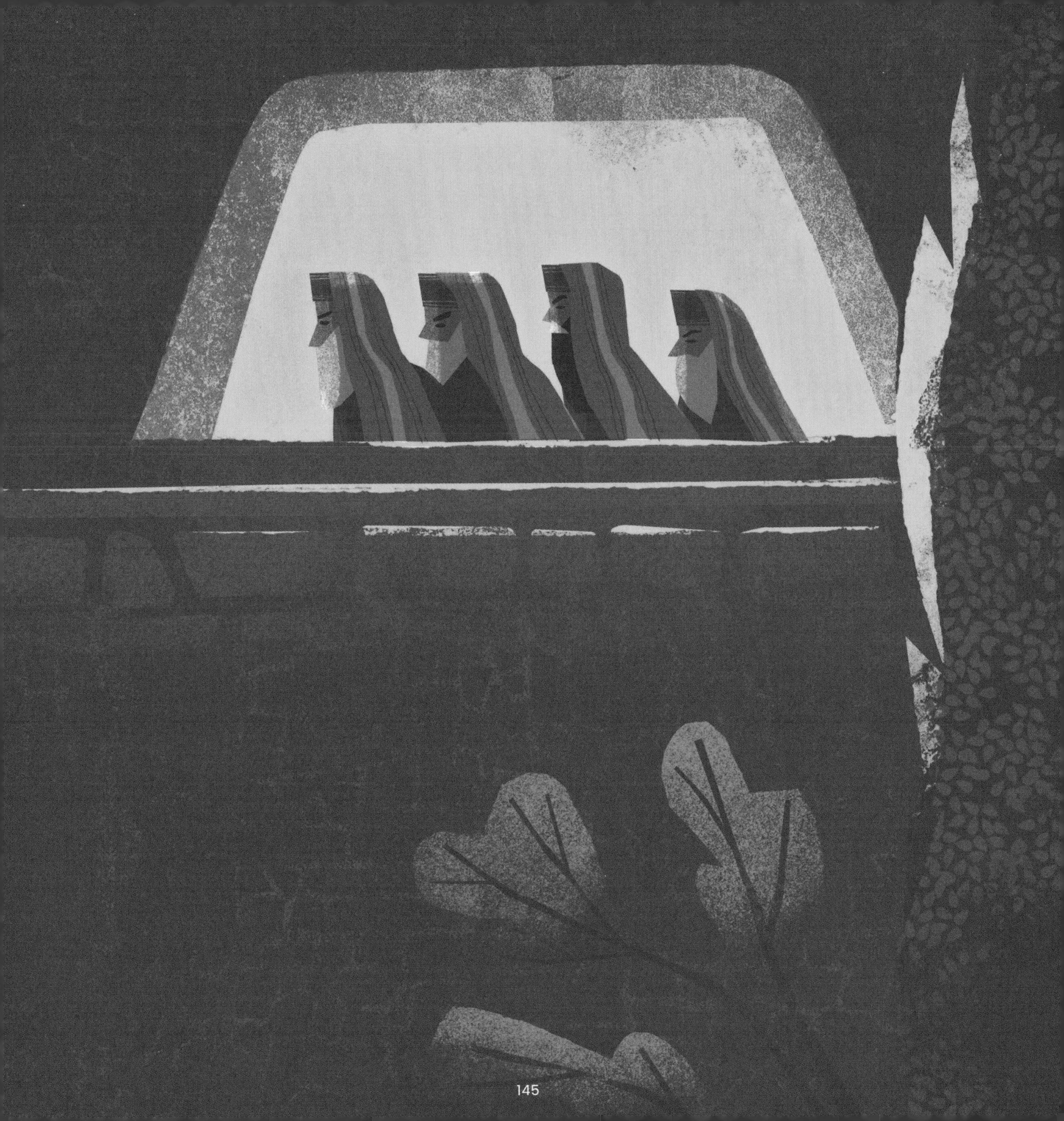

Hours pass...

Dawn begins to break over the eastern hills...

Now, you are following as they walk Him across the city, still in chains, toward the place from which the Roman governor rules the land.

Are they taking Him to Pontius Pilate? you wonder to yourself. *How can this be? Only criminals are taken to him!*

Yet in they lead Him through the high iron gate and into the inner shadowy courtyard behind those big gray walls. Above you now, is the governor's balcony. On it, at its center, is the judgment seat. You're following the temple guard—and Jesus—in the midst of a curious crowd of onlookers. It seems like all Jerusalem is suddenly around you.

And now He's being led up, up, up a flight of stairs, past the judgment seat and into Pilate's inner offices. The crowd waits outside, as the minutes pass. Then it's hours. The morning passes...

Until, suddenly, a different side door opens into the courtyard and the guards are dragging a prisoner past you and back up the stairs to the judgment seat. You have never seen a person look like this...

From head to toe, the Man is covered in cuts and bruises and gashes and blood, but, strangely, He is also wearing a purple king's robe. And, even more strangely, a crown—you look closer—it's a crown made of long horrible thorns.

And as He's passing past the crowd and you watch Him, so sad for whoever He is, suddenly He glances over at you...

It is Him!

It is *Jesus!*

Yet, even still, even after being whipped and beaten up and mocked by the soldiers, His eyes are lit up with peace—and joy. He nods His head at you: He still knows what He's doing.

You start to cry as you watch Him...

In just another minute, they have brought Him to the top of the stairs, up above the crowd, and He's standing now next to Pilate. They are standing behind a railing, just in front of the judgment seat, and they're facing down toward you and all the people.

Suddenly, Pilate raises his hand. The crowd grows instantly quiet.

"So," he says, "I have taught this Man a lesson and now it's time to hand Him back to you. He's done nothing wrong."

"No! No! No!" the people shout around you. "Kill Him! Kill Him!"

"For what *reason*?" Pilate asks, and you can see that he is growing troubled by this whole experience.

"Kill him! Kill him!" the crowd continues to yell and scream. "Crucify! Crucify!"

The look on Pilate's face is almost frightened now; you can see how he glances over, time and again, at Jesus.

And then you look at Jesus for yourself. He has been watching you, waiting for you to look.

The edge of His lip suddenly turns up, just a little, into that hint of a smile that always used to light His face.

Slowly, He nods His head at you. You are looking at His eyes with every ounce of your energy.

In His eyes are peace... and joy.

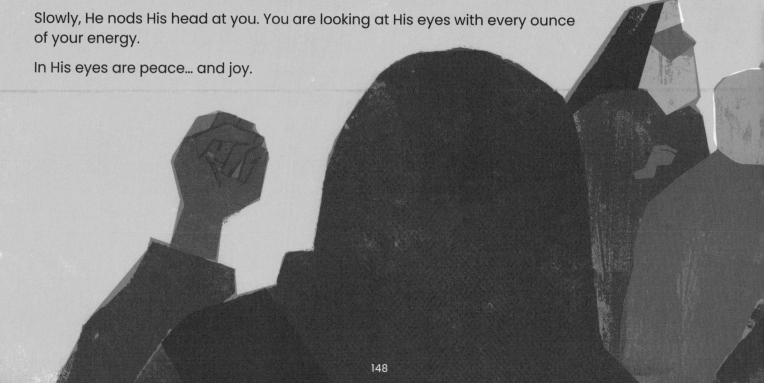

He knows exactly what He's doing, you realize.

You stand amidst the crowd and you
watch Him as they put a cross upon Him.
He begins to walk the road to Calvary.

Let's Talk About It

Why do you think Jesus felt peace and joy even when He was being arrested and beaten?

What did He know that the crowds didn't?

Chapter 16

Today in Paradise

Luke 23:26-43

Imagine if you were a criminal. A terrible criminal. Imagine if, all the way back to your earliest memories of your youngest youth, you'd only ever done the wrong thing. In fact, ever since you can remember, the only thing you'd ever *wanted* to do was the exact wrong thing. As a little child, you would steal your friends' lunches. You would ask for money and never plan to pay it back. You would wait till no one was watching and kick friendly animals. You would sneak out of your house and do terrible acts of mischief...

And things only got worse as you got older, got bigger, got smarter, got tougher, got meaner. Now, you looked for new and different opportunities to break the law: you were always trying to do something worse than last time...

All in all, you became a very bad person. You became a very *hard* person.

So, eventually, when you found yourself arrested, put in jail, put on trial, you began to feel feelings you'd never really felt before. You felt a sense of guilt. You felt shame. You felt like whatever sentence you might receive might just be the sentence you actually deserve...

And when that Roman judge decided what your fate was—DEATH!—you weren't particularly surprised or bewildered. It seemed to you that dying on a cross was the natural ending for a life of very unnatural living. It seemed to you that this was actually what you deserved. It seemed—somehow—right...

And now you're up upon that hill—the hill called "Skull" or "Calvary"—and the terrible day of your execution has arrived. And now they're stretching out your arms and legs to be nailed to the cross, and—

OH! the pain is OVERWHELMING!

You scream a scream of endless agony. All the people watching laugh at you.

And now they're lifting up your cross and now—OH! – it has dropped into the hole they've dug to keep it standing upright. And you are gasping now to gather up each breath as all your body weight is sagging down, hanging against the pain of the nails.

And that's when you look around for just a second...

You are looking around at the world you are leaving...

You are looking at the blue sky overhead, the hills in the distance, the city—white and brown—standing down below. You look at all the faces of the scoffers and the soldiers and the citizens who are simply walking by...

And then you turn your head to the right, to your side, to regard the other criminals who are being killed next to you...

And that's when you see Him.

A Man you have certainly heard much about.

A Man who everyone once said might be the Savior, the King of Kings, the long-awaited Messiah of your people...

What is He doing here? you wonder to yourself. *He is not the sort of Man to end up here...*

And that's when He turns to look at *you*.

And something happens down inside you.

You have never experienced love, understanding, human kindness—and now you see them all in those eyes. His eyes are regarding you. His eyes are *accepting* you.

But, suddenly, *"Hey! Aren't you a savior? Why don't you save yourself and us?"* echoes from the other side of Jesus. You recognize that voice; it is the other condemned man, one of a gang of criminals you used to run with...

But you say to him, "Don't you understand? We are getting exactly what our crimes deserve here. But this Man has never done a wrong thing ever..."

There is something in the eyes of Jesus that tells your heart that what He's doing is purposeful, needed, necessary. His eyes speak of hope... peace... joy.

And now you're calling up every bit of all your courage and your hope and your heart to be brave enough to speak His name:

"Jesus?"

He turns His head to look at you.

"Remember me," you whisper, "when you come into your Kingdom."

You watch how He gently smiles.

Then He leans His head as close as He can get to you, pulling against the nails, and you'll never forget what He says to you:

"Truly I tell you," He says, *"today* you will be with Me in Paradise."

Today.

In Paradise.

You find yourself believing Him.

You find yourself believing in Jesus.

And now, you say to your heart, you may die happy.

You may die free.

Jesus, the Teacher, the Messiah, the Savior of the world, is dying to *set you free.*

Let's Talk About It

Have you ever done something wrong that you regretted later?
How did that feel?

What does it feel like to be forgiven and loved even after you've done
something wrong?

What does it feel like to forgive someone else when they hurt you?

Chapter 17

The Great Surprise

Matthew 28:1-10, Mark 16:1-7, Luke 24:1-11, John 20:1-18

Imagine the greatest feeling of surprise you could ever imagine. That feeling down in your stomach as you gasp with amazement. The way your mouth pops open—*WHOA!*—in absolute shock. How your body *JUMPS* because you're almost scared right then. How you feel your heart start racing with disbelief…

Well, we're not there yet.

Not quite.

So, first, imagine instead you're walking in the very early, not-yet-sunrise morning through the mist and coolness of the outskirts of a big city. Just a few minutes ago, you passed by the last of the houses and buildings and streets; now you're in the countryside, walking farther and farther out. You are going to visit your friend's grave this morning. You are going to pay your last respects to your best friend, Jesus.

As you're almost to the place where you saw them put His body on Friday—the cave with the stone out front—you start to feel a bit nervous. The mist and darkness make the place feel haunted and almost scary; the shadows and silence suddenly seem very large.

And that's when the ground around you begins to shake...

Along with the trees and the rocks and the hills: *an earthquake!*

You do your best to stay on your feet as the earth shakes beneath you. You stumble and roll and move right along with the earth's surface.

Finally, it stops.

All is quiet.

Now, all the *more* scared, you begin again walking closer toward the tomb through the shadows and the stillness and the morning mist...

And that's the moment you see the glowing man...

sitting on the stone rolled away from the mouth of the grave...

And this glowing man seems to be waiting for *you!*

Down below him, a group of Roman soldiers are lying in the dust and dirt; they seem as if knocked out by the power of this man on the rolled-away stone. And there, next to him, the opening of Jesus' tomb is actually OPEN; your stomach starts to twist in knots of fear and shock...

The glowing man smiles at you.

"Do not be afraid," he says. "I know that you are here to say goodbye to your friend, Jesus. You saw Him die on the cross on Friday, didn't you? Well, He isn't here anymore..."

And even before you have the chance to ask where He is, the man—an angel?—continues to explain: "He is risen, just like He said He would! Go ahead. Take a look. See inside the tomb where He *was*. And then run on back to the city and tell His friends that *He's alive*."

And you are so completely overwhelmed by this idea—the idea that Jesus is actually alive—that you *don't* go inside the tomb to investigate. No, you turn on your heel and begin running through the garden toward the city: you must go and tell His disciples this strange news!

Out ahead, the fresh light of dawn is starting to break and shine through the mist; everything looks hazy and new and golden to you. You're weaving your way through trees and flowers and bushes, trying to find the path back to the city, when, suddenly—

You run into a Man!

You hadn't even seen Him there in the dawning of the golden light.

"Why are you crying?" this Man asks you.

His face is hidden by the silhouetting of the sun behind Him. You try to explain yourself to this shadowy Stranger: "Because I'm so confused," you say. "I came here looking for my friend, Jesus, and now that shining man says He's gone. I don't know what to believe..."

And then the wildest thing in your whole life happens...

This Stranger standing in the golden mist speaks your name!

He whispers it across the distance hanging between you with all the love and warm affection of that voice you know so well...

This Stranger is...

Jesus!

Alive!

And He's standing right in front of you!

Just as surely as you'd seen Him dead on Friday, you are seeing Him on Sunday morning—alive and Himself!

Jesus!

Alive!

You run to Him and throw yourself before Him and hug His legs... this is really real... it is really Him... He is really Jesus! He has the same aroma, the same presence, the same exact Self: it is really, truly Jesus you are holding onto!

"Peace be with you!" He says, laughing. You look up into His face and He is smiling down right at you. "Now go and tell my brothers and sisters— tell the world—that I am going to the Father, to *your* Father, to my God, to *your* God..."

But all you want to do is hold onto Him now.

Because, He is alive!

REALLY ALIVE!

Let's Talk About It

How do you think the disciples felt when they realized that Jesus, who had died, was now alive?

Why do you think Mary didn't recognize Him right away?

Chapter 18

A Walk & A Shock

Luke 24:13-33a

Imagine walking along a straight, narrow, dusty road in the country, having a chat with one of your best friends. It is the middle of the late afternoon. You are walking at a comfortable pace; you are listening to your friend as you look out over the scenery. Low orangish-brownish hills stretch off to your left; to your right, there is a plain that goes on and on until it meets the distant horizon. You have been deep in thought all afternoon—all day, in fact—and you're deep in thought about the same things your friend is speaking of.

"I just don't understand," he is saying to you. "I've always trusted Mary's judgment before. And now it seems as if John is believing it too."

Your friend is talking about the strange sorts of happenings that have been occuring all day today, and you run them over in your mind:

Mary's tale of the earthquake, the angel, the *supposed* sighting of Jesus in the morning mist...

Peter and John's running out to the tomb in the dawning half-light and John's certainty now that *He is alive*...

The whispers in the streets that all the soldiers saw *something*, saw *someone*, and that the authorities have paid them off...

Turning it all over in your mind, you just have no idea *what* to think, *what* to believe, *what* to hope, *what* to dream...

And that's when you start to notice the crunching sound of someone's sandals on the road, just behind you. He is walking rather fast. He is almost catching up to you. And as He draws near, He matches you in step and starts to walk beside you—so you glance over. His cloak has a hood, which He has pulled up over His head, so you can only just see the tip of His nose.

174

"What are you two talking about?" He asks. "It seems like something pretty serious."

You and your friend both stop. What a strange way for a stranger to start a conversation!

You say: "You must be the only person in Jerusalem who hasn't heard of all the things that have been happening recently!"

The Stranger laughs to Himself. *Did He really just laugh?* you think.

"What things?" asks the Stranger, with amusement. The three of you begin walking together.

"Oh, about Jesus of Nazareth," your friend replies. "Now there was a Man—a prophet so amazingly powerful in word and deed that we'd hoped He was the Savior. Have you really not heard a word about His life and about His death and about the rumors that He really was the King of Kings?"

"Perhaps I've heard something about Him," the Stranger says.

Your friend continues talking: "And if all that wasn't enough, now it's almost been three days since He was killed, and some strange things have been happening. Some of our friends went to the tomb this morning, couldn't find His body, say they saw an angel—and we simply don't know what to believe."

The Stranger walks along in silence for a moment. Then He clears His throat.

"Well," He says, "is it possible that you both are just a little slow to believe all that was meant to happen to that Man? Didn't the prophets say He *must* die? Didn't He Himself proclaim that He would return? Really, wasn't it the exact plan of God that the Savior needed to die for His people and, in that way, find His glory?"

What sort of Stranger is this? you're thinking to yourself. And yet He just keeps talking...

Now, He's talking about the Creation of the whole world: how God created all we see in order that we should see Him. And He talks about the sad story of Adam and of Eve: how all humankind was sickened with the disease called Sin. And He talks about the Israelites, the Promised Land, the Tabernacle and the Temple— it's amazing all the things He knows! He talks about the prophets like He *knows* them—like He's *met* them before—and He talks of them with so much power...

After a long time, you're suddenly aware that you are almost home—home to your little house in your little village of Emmaus. The afternoon has now fully come and gone; the evening colors paint the cloudy westward sky in pinks and purples.

You're just about to make a turn to your house.

You're just about to say goodnight to your friend.

And that's the moment when you realize that the Stranger will keep on walking into the darkness; He is not stopping here with you. *But He must stop here,* you think. *The road beyond is not so safe in the nighttime...*

So, you invite Him into your home, along with your friend, and now you're walking through the quiet streets toward your front door. The three of you go in together.

You light a candle, take a loaf of bread from the shelf, open a bottle of wine, and set the table for your two friends. Everything looks perfect.

You sit down across from the Stranger.

With a gentle move, the Stranger lifts both hands and pulls back the hood of His cloak from His head. Then He reaches over—over toward the glowing candlelight—and He picks up the loaf of bread you laid out. He begins to pray:

"Father," He says, "I am grateful for the journey I've taken today with these two friends. What a blessing they've been to me! Now would you bless them both with eyes to see? Amen and Amen."

And as you hear Him break the bread and as you watch Him leaning forward to pass it over, His face is suddenly lit up. The glowing of the yellow candlelight catches across His features, the features of—

Jesus!

The Stranger is Jesus!

And just as quickly as that thought has crossed your mind, He is gone—*vanished!*—and you and your friend now sit in absolute silence.

But now you know for yourself: He is alive!

You run out the door to tell the others...

All must know!

Let's Talk About It

Have you ever had a hard time believing something someone told you? Is it easier for you to believe things that people tell you about or things that you see for yourself?

How do you think it would have felt to realize that you'd been walking and talking with Jesus the whole time?

Chapter 19

Up Into the Clouds

Acts 1:4-11

Imagine the loveliest day for having a picnic. It's the sort of day where light, fluffy clouds cruise the blue skies; where the sun is just so perfectly warm, not too hot. You are sitting on the brow of a hill, looking back toward the city, and you're resting on a soft comfortable blanket. You're surrounded by all your best and closest friends. You've just finished eating; you lean back and enjoy all your pleasant feelings.

You close your eyes and listen to the singing of a bird; he is trilling and hooting with delight that he is alive. You are feeling the gentle breeze across your face. You are happy and content with the fact that *you* are alive. Although He is across from you on the picnic blanket, you still can't quite believe that Jesus is with you, that He's been amongst you for these forty days now. Far happier than the bird's song and the joy of your own little life, is this glorious wonder that *Jesus is alive!*

You just can't shake the amazement of the whole thing.

Suddenly, He speaks up: "You have already heard me talk about this before," He is saying, "about how John the Baptist used to baptize people with water. Do you remember that? Well, in not too many days, all of *you* will be baptized with something else: the Holy Spirit."

You and your friends lean closer, curious.

Someone asks, "So, does that mean that *this* is the time when you are going to become the King of Israel? Is it soon that you'll defeat the Romans?"

Jesus smiles softly. He leans back upon His elbows.

"My friends, it's not for you to know the times and dates and ins and outs of my Father's plan; not yet, at least..."

Then His eyes narrow sharply: He is looking into your eyes with the most serious sort of expression on His face.

"But *you*," He says—and it's almost like He's only speaking to *you* now—"will be given power when the Holy Spirit arrives. And *you* will be my witness, not only in this nearby town, or this nearby country, or the next one over—*No!*—you will be my witness to everyone everywhere."

And even as those words are ringing in your ears and you are wondering about their meaning, the most marvelous thing in the whole world is happening. A downward blast of wind begins to blow. The sunlight starts to shine with extra brilliance. And now, Jesus is suddenly lifting up—up from the blanket and the ground and the earth and from all of you. He is actually starting to rise up—up above your picnic and this hillside and your circle of friends. He is rising higher and higher and swifter and swifter now—He is almost at the level of those light fluffy clouds...

And then, suddenly, His rising slows...

For a moment, He is suspended there, high in the air...

And He is looking right at you and, just for the space of a moment, His eyes remind you of the adventures you have shared together. Of walking over the hills and the plains together. Of the many, many miracles you have seen Him do. Of the wonderful teachings and stories He has spoken. Of all your inside jokes and shared sense of humor.

And, of course, you cannot help but think of how He died to set you free: all the pain He endured to give you life forever. And oh! how His eyes are twinkling still with the light of His Resurrection: He is ever alive and always, forever, will be!

And then, just like that, just as all these wonderful memories are passing between you, He is suddenly gone. Ascended into the clouds.

But you have a sneaking suspicion that you'll see Him again.

There's something in your heart that knows: *This is not the end*.

Let's Talk About It

Why do we need the Holy Spirit to do all of the things that Jesus has told us to do?

Close your eyes and use your imagination to picture a very special place that you and Jesus can go together. What is it like there? What is Jesus doing? What kinds of things is Jesus saying to you?

Chapter 20

What Happens Next

Acts 2:1-4

Imagine you've only just left that hilltop—only just finished seeing Jesus disappear into the clouds—and now you're back in the room you'd left earlier. This is the very same room where He'd washed all your feet, from which He'd gone to the Garden of Gethsemane. This is the room where you've been meeting since He rose from the dead. Your heart and mind are overwhelmed—*astounded!*—by His ascending up to Heaven; you fall into a chair and simply stare across the room.

Your eyes slowly move across the tabletop in front of you until—*look at that!*—you notice His cloak, lying right there. His best one. His favorite.

You pick it up and sit back in your chair again. You hold the cloak to your face. It smells like Him...

"Should we pray?" someone asks.

Everyone agrees—yes, we should...

So you bow your heads—perfect silence...

"O Eternal God," one of your friends begins, "thou art worthy of our greatest professions of love and honor and—"

He stops. Perhaps something has distracted him. Perhaps he's missing Jesus, or feeling confused, or suddenly scared—or simply doesn't know what to say when speaking directly to the Father.

Then the same voice begins again, but quietly:

"*Jesus?* It's us. All of us."

You are listening to the very first time in all human history when someone has approached Heaven by talking to your friend Jesus. It makes your eyes suddenly fill up with tears. *We can still talk to Him!* you realize, rejoicing...

And now imagine you are in that very same room, just ten days later, surrounded by all the same friends, all the same furniture, all the same feelings of wonder. For these last ten days, almost all you've done is talk to Jesus; it's the only thing all of you *want* to do anymore! This experience in your heart and mind is *almost as good* as being with Him. You can all agree that talking to Him is like Heaven on earth...

And that's when this wild thing begins to happen...

The sound of a violent wind within the house...

You open your eyes to see if a breeze has blown the windows open—what in the world is happening?—and that's when you see them...

Bright dashes of an orange and red flame.

Little bits of heavenly fire circling the room.

They seem to be descending from above you and they hover over the heads of everyone in the room. Their presence is like a visit of Heaven itself. You're not sure what to do—or to think...

When, suddenly, one of them disappears down upon you—*and within you!*—and your whole heart and mind and spirit are lit up like a flame! Warmth spreads within your inner life like fire. The whole experience of your inner world explodes with power. It's like you used to have walls that shut up everything inside you, that fenced your heart in, that kept your life feeling nice and normal...

And now those walls are gone forever: *demolished!* Your inner life is just as wide open, as wild, as His! There is nothing now to separate you from experiencing *all* of Jesus, *all* of the Father, *all* of the Holy Spirit!

And that's the moment when you realize what's happened to you...

That's when you actually understand...

Ten days ago, before He went up to Heaven, Jesus had said: "You will be given power when *the Holy Spirit* comes upon you."

This is the Holy Spirit! you realize. *The Spirit of Jesus has come to live inside me!*

And then the most wonderful thought—the highest and best possible thought for every man, woman and child—occurs to you:

"Holy Spirit, what does Jesus want me to do *next*?"

That's the question you can enjoy for the rest of your life.

Let's Talk About It

How do you like to talk to Jesus? What do you like to talk about?

How do you experience the Holy Spirit—in your body, or a nice and peaceful feeling in your heart, or is it something else?

How do you hear Jesus' voice? What kinds of things does He like to tell you? Ask Him if there is something He wants to tell you today!

Afterword

From Bill Johnson

The wonder and imagination of children are gifts from their Creator. These encounters with Jesus they've just experienced do not need to stop with this book. Rather, now that you have read through these powerful *Moments with Jesus* with the children in your life, let them act as a springboard for your child's own encounters with God.

As they read through their Bibles, allow them to imagine their own moments: What would it have been like to be a young David, preparing your sling for Goliath? What would it have felt like to know that your brothers were against you, but that God was on your side? How would it have felt to take down the enemy of Israel? The Bible is filled with stories of God showing who He is and what He is like to His people. And that hasn't changed.

There is no junior Holy Spirit. God's desire to speak to them, reveal Himself to them, give them encounters with Him is in no way less than His desire to connect with adults. We can encourage our children and grandchildren to explore their relationship with God in ways that are tangible and real. If Jesus was that kind, understanding, and loving to His disciples, what do you think He thinks about that situation your child is facing at school? How would He encourage your child when they're facing disappointment or sadness? What kinds of things would He laugh with them about? Jesus is real, active, and alive.

He is the one who has written their destinies, who designed them with gifts and purpose, who invites them to impact the course of history. Representing Him on the earth, we adults have a role to play in shaping the world by how we love, serve, and minister to children.

About Bill Johnson

Bill Johnson is a fifth-generation pastor with a rich heritage in the Holy Spirit. Bill and his wife, Beni, are the senior leaders of Bethel Church in Redding, California, and serve a growing number of churches that cross denominational lines, demonstrate power, and partner for revival. Bill's vision is for all believers to experience God's presence and operate in the miraculous—as expressed in his bestselling books *When Heaven Invades Earth* and *Hosting the Presence*. The Johnsons have three children and ten grandchildren.

About Eugene Luning

Eugene Luning directs The Union, a ministry within the New Horizons Foundation, which exists for teaching, retreats, podcasting, and spiritual counseling in Colorado and around the country. Additionally, he is the cofounder of a real estate technology company, Panoramiq Markets Inc.

Eugene and his wife Jenny are the parents of three children, Hadley, Tripp, and Hoyt. They live in Colorado Springs, Colorado, where they also lead a weekly fellowship, The Anchor.

About Kevin & Kristen Howdeshell

Kevin & Kristen Howdeshell are a husband and wife team illustrating a variety of projects including bestselling children's books, food packaging, movie posters, music albums, and editorial spots. Their work is characterized with texture, a mid-century influence, and a lean toward meaningful family time. They lead up The Brave Union Studio in Kansas City, Missouri where they raise their three young kids, and enjoy their Betta fish, their treehouse, and trampoline. In their non-art hours, Kevin enjoys fly fishing, Kristen likes working in the yard while listening to a baseball game, and both enjoy playing board games with the kids. Follow their work @TheBraveUnion on Instagram.

About the Moments with Jesus Project

The Moments with Jesus Project is committed to helping children and adults encounter Jesus for themselves by engaging Scripture through the power of imagination.

To this end, we offer resources including books, podcasts, videos, and more.

Learn more by visiting our website:
www.momentswithjesusproject.com

Or connect with us on social media:
@momentswithjesusproject

the
BILL JOHNSON
collection

Bill Johnson

**Moments with Jesus
Encounter Bible**

The King's Way of Life

God is Really Good

Open Heavens

**Mornings and
Evenings in His
Presence**

The Way of Life

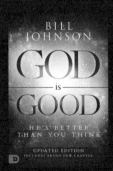

God is Good

**When Heaven
Invades Earth**

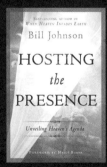

**Hosting the
Presence**

DESTINY IMAGE *Bethel*